James E. Hunter

COVER PHOTOGRAPHY:	Jim Harrison
FOREWORD:	Bill Davis
AUTHOR:	James E. Hunter
PHOTOGRAPHY:	See Credits
PUBLISHER & EDITOR:	H. Donald Kroitzsh
DESIGNER:	Ondrea J. Beckett
ASSISTANT EDITORS:	Anne C. Pace-Rosa Ondrea J. Beckett Lou Chap Barbara A. Ritchotte

Printed and bound in Canada

Published by:
Five Corners Publications, Ltd.
HCR 70 Box 2
Plymouth, Vermont 05056
USA

The Curiosity Book
ISBN: 1-886699-04-6

Foreword

Enlightening...Insightful...Compassionate...Courageous. These are some of the attributes which, in my judgment, describe *The Curiosity Book.* Calling upon his diverse and rich professional experience with children and adolescents, the author, James Hunter, has developed a unique and extremely practical guide which should be of invaluable help to both parents and a wide range of professionals within the mental health and education fields. *The Curiosity Book* is written with a great deal of sensitivity and respect for the human body itself and, more importantly, the need to promote positive attitudes involving the human body.

It is ironic that while most of us in today's society who consider ourselves to be caring adults frequently encourage children to be curious about their learning, their environment, and their friends, we, at the same time, typically discourage, ignore, or even punish children when they express curiosity about the human body — their own or others. Thus, many children learn to view this type of curiosity as *bad or as shameful. The Curiosity Book* provides specific, sensitive suggestions whereby parents and child care professionals can engage in effective, healthy *communication* with children about the human body — developmentally, attitudinally, and spiritually.

The photos contained in this book have been carefully selected to convey tolerant, respectful, and meaningful messages. They are inspiring and beautiful both in their simplicity and in their poignancy. As is the case with the narrative material contained in this work, the photos reflect a very well-balanced perspective relative to attitudes involving the human body — age, gender, and cultural diversity.

I enthusiastically recommend *The Curiosity Book* to all parents and to all professionals in their efforts to help children develop more positive attitudes toward, and a more respectful appreciation of, the human body.

William E. Davis, PhD
Director of the Institute for the Study of Children At Risk
University of Maine
Orono, Maine
January 1997

And God saw everything that He had made,
and behold, it was very good.
Genesis 1:31
From Delight all these beings are born,
by Delight they exist and grow,
to Delight they return.
Taittirya Upanishad

The Curiosity Book and Its Use

An Introduction for Parents, Educators, Counselors, and Other Child Care Workers.

The Curiosity Book **is about helping children acquire positive attitudes, healthy habits, and useful information about the human body. In its original form, it was developed in a mental health clinic for use by mental health professionals in their work with elementary school age children. Hoping that the clinical expertise that was gained with this population might be of use to a much wider readership, the original concept was expanded. The intended result is a book that will be useful to the general population of children and their parents, teachers, counselors and other caregivers.**

The Curiosity Book **grows out of, and reflects, certain fundamental value commitments. The author believes that the human body is an integral aspect of a good creation. Rightly used, the body is a source of joy; a crucible for personal and spiritual development; a vehicle for the love, affection and nurturing that facilitate deep human attachment, and an abode of the Ultimate Mystery.**

Awareness of our bodies should not be associated with shame. No one should be belittled for any physical attribute. Children should not be made ashamed of their curiosity any more than they should be ashamed of their bodies. ***The Curiosity Book*** **affirms the value of open discussion of matters pertaining to the body.**

People in our society from birth onward generally have a need for much more physical intimacy than they receive. Therefore, ***The Curiosity Book*** **celebrates the value of touch.**

Finally, ***The Curiosity Book*** **is committed to the creation of a world which protects every child's right to be safe from physical, economic, sexual, or emotional abuse or exploitation.**

Although children might benefit from looking through it by themselves, ***The Curiosity Book*** **was prepared specifically for adults and children to read together. The adult might be a teacher, a relative, a counselor, or a friend. Parents, however, are the child's first and most important educators. It is therefore especially appropriate for them to read** ***The Curiosity Book*** **with their children.**

As parents teach facts and satisfy their child's natural curiosity, they

may find that this is the optimal time to convey to the child their family's values, rules and customs. Parents are encouraged to teach what they believe. Children benefit from clear guidelines. They need to understand and identify with the values and customs of their family. Parents are encouraged to take a positive approach. While negative practices may need to be identified, the central thrust of the discussion should be on the values that are being affirmed.

Whether we are mental health professionals, parents, teachers or just interested bystanders, most of us have some uncertainties about which progressive ideas really represent progress, and which conservative principles truly merit conservation. There are no easy answers. Dialogue is probably the key for making headway. Therefore, it is suggested that anybody planning to use this book first sit down with his or her spouse, with extended family members, with friends, with a professional mentor, and/or with a spiritual guide, and discuss some of the crucial questions. What are the limits of good touch? When is it appropriate to be seen naked, or to see someone else naked? To what extent should children share the parent's bed? What are the appropriate times and circumstances for explicit sexual behavior? What range of freedom should be permitted to children with regard to sexual play and experimentation? These are not easy questions in today's world.

A certain amount of suspicion and mistrust exists between parents and mental health professionals. Neither the causes nor the solutions to this problem are simple, but again, dialogue is probably the key to making progress. We strongly urge parents, educators and mental health workers to talk with one another. Specifically we encourage any educator or mental health worker who is thinking about using *The Curiosity Book* to sit down with parents and show it to them, explaining its purpose with the child, and describing its use. Whenever I have done this, I have received positive responses even with very "conservative" parents.

The Curiosity Book affirms that appropriate rules and norms must guide our behavior in this sphere of life. Modern sex education has at times been lax in teaching appropriate rules of conduct along with the facts. Individual growth and social harmony are not fostered by anarchy. Yet we do not wish to resurrect the repressive attitudes, harsh judgmental approaches, and secretive practices that have harmed so many people in our society. Above all we must avoid conveying the attitude that the body itself, and the things it can do, are intrinsically unwholesome, dirty or shameful.

In dealing with rules and morality it should be made clear to the child that no feelings are, in themselves, moral or immoral. Our feelings are just our feelings. The same is true of our thoughts. Morality has to do with what we DO with our feelings and our thoughts. It is about BEHAVIOR.

It is important to empower our children to protect themselves from older people who would exploit them sexually. It is also important to facilitate emotional healing in those children who have had unfortunate experiences of a sexual nature. *The Curiosity Book* targets both of these issues. Yet in our concern to protect our children from sexual abuse and its consequences, we must not be pushed into hysterical and extreme reactions that can be as harmful as the abuse. In homes, schools and communities across the country people have become afraid to touch, hug and cuddle children. This is unfortunate. All children need to be held; those who have been mistreated perhaps even more so than others. The corrective experience for having been sexually or physically abused is not the avoidance of touching; it is warm, affectionate, non-exploitive touching.

Masturbation is a common concern for parents. Most child care workers believe that masturbation is almost universal among children. Certainly it is very common. This is a harmless activity that can generally be ignored by adults. In some cases children may need reassurance that if they play with themselves, it is not shameful or bad. On the other hand it is private. Some children might need guidance from an adult with regard to the times, places and situations in which masturbation is appropriate.

Parents and child care workers are encouraged to give some thought to the setting in which they want to share *The Curiosity Book* with the children under their care. In the home the first three rules are turn the TV off, turn the TV off, and turn the TV off. Then find a cozy place to sit down. Side by side on a couch is good, or the child may want to sit on your lap. A shared snack will add immeasurably to the atmosphere.

Above all else *The Curiosity Book* intends to open communication between the child's caregivers and the child. I would suggest going through the book in a relaxed and leisurely manner, pausing often for discussion. If the child is anxious to see all the pictures, an alternate approach is to read through the book a first time fairly rapidly, and then return to dwell on each section with greater care. Adults are encouraged to experiment and do what works, keeping in mind that the greatest benefit from the book is derived from the leisurely, thoughtful and respectful discussion that it stimulates.

The Curiosity Book should be used flexibly, dealing with those questions and issues that naturally arise as an adult and a child share the book together. However, I would suggest some possible questions that, at different points in the book, might be used for stimulating discussion:

It's O.K. to be curious.

What things are you curious about?

Is there anything special about bodies you have been curious about?

People don't all look the same.

What kind of differences have you noticed about people and their bodies?

Do you ever hear grown ups or other kids saying bad things about others' bodies?

What do you think about this?

We are all beautiful.

Whom do you find especially beautiful?

Why?

Are there different ways of being beautiful?

Do you think you are beautiful?

What do you especially like about your body?

Do you think your grandmother is beautiful?

What about your baby brother?

Does everybody find the same things beautiful?

We can do many wonderful things with our bodies.

What are some of the fun things you like to do with your body?

What can you do that you are proud of?

There are rules about bodies.

What are our family's rules?

Do these seem like good rules?
Do you ever see people breaking important rules?
Do you think most people break some rules sometimes?
What can we do if we have broken an important rule?

One special thing bodies are for is having and caring for children.
Where do babies come from?
What is our belly button for?
How do mamas feed babies?

I hope that reading *The Curiosity Book* will provide an occasion for the fruitful examination of the values of the adults, and for in-depth discussion regarding the behavioral guidelines that support those values. With this preparation, reading *The Curiosity Book* with a child will provide an opportunity to convey some of the highest values of our society to our children.

James E. Hunter

Curiosity is, in great and generous minds, the first passion and the last.

Samuel Johnson

To all the children and their caregivers with whom I have worked

The Children's Section

Most often we wear clothes

Even when sleeping...

or going swimming, most people wear some clothes.

LAGUNA

In some places people don't wear so many clothes. It seems natural to them.

Kids sometimes wonder what people look like without their clothes.

NATIONAL GEOGRAPHIC
MOGULS
ISLE ROYALE—
NORTH WOODS
PARK PRIMEVAL

This is called curiosity.

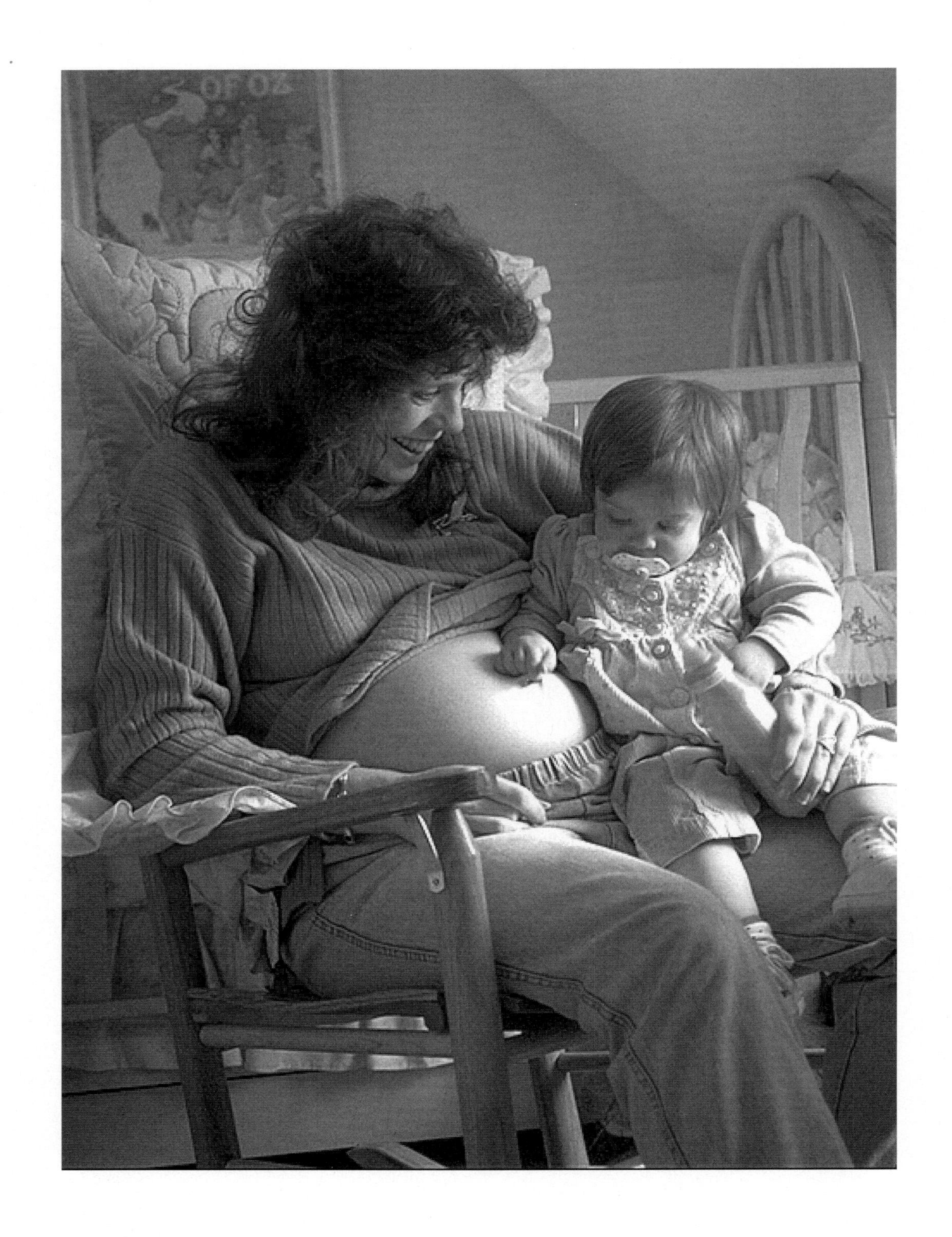

It's OK to be curious.

This face you got,
This here phizzog you carry around,
You never picked it out for yourself,
at all, at all — did you?

Carl Sandburg

People don't all look the same.

They come in different sizes...

Different shapes...

HOMAGE TO ZUÑIGA
FELIPE CASTEÑADA
GIFT OF
MRS. BRADFORD WHITTEMORE
MRS. RICHARD HARRISON HILL

different colors.

Boys look one way...

and girls another.

Women look different from men.

Children look different from grown-ups.

Older people look different from younger people.

My heart leaps up when I behold
A rainbow in the sky:
So was it when my life began;
So is it now I am a man;
So be it when I shall grow old...

William Wordsworth

But we are all beautiful just as God created us.

We can do many wonderful things with our bodies.

What are days for?
Days are where we live.
They come, they wake us
Time and time over.
They are to be happy in:
Where can we live but days?

Philip Larkin

God laughs and plays.

Meister Eckhart

> *He was only a fox,*
> *like a hundred other foxes*
> *But I have made him my friend,*
> *and now he is unique in all the world.*
>
> **Antoine de Saint-Exupery**

One thing we can do with our bodies is show our love for each other with hugs, kisses, and cuddling. We all need lots of this kind of touching.

Also grown-ups need to touch children to help them dress and bathe.

I would like to sing someone to sleep,
have someone to sit by and be with.
I would like to cradle you and softly sing,
be your companion while you sleep or wake.

Rilke

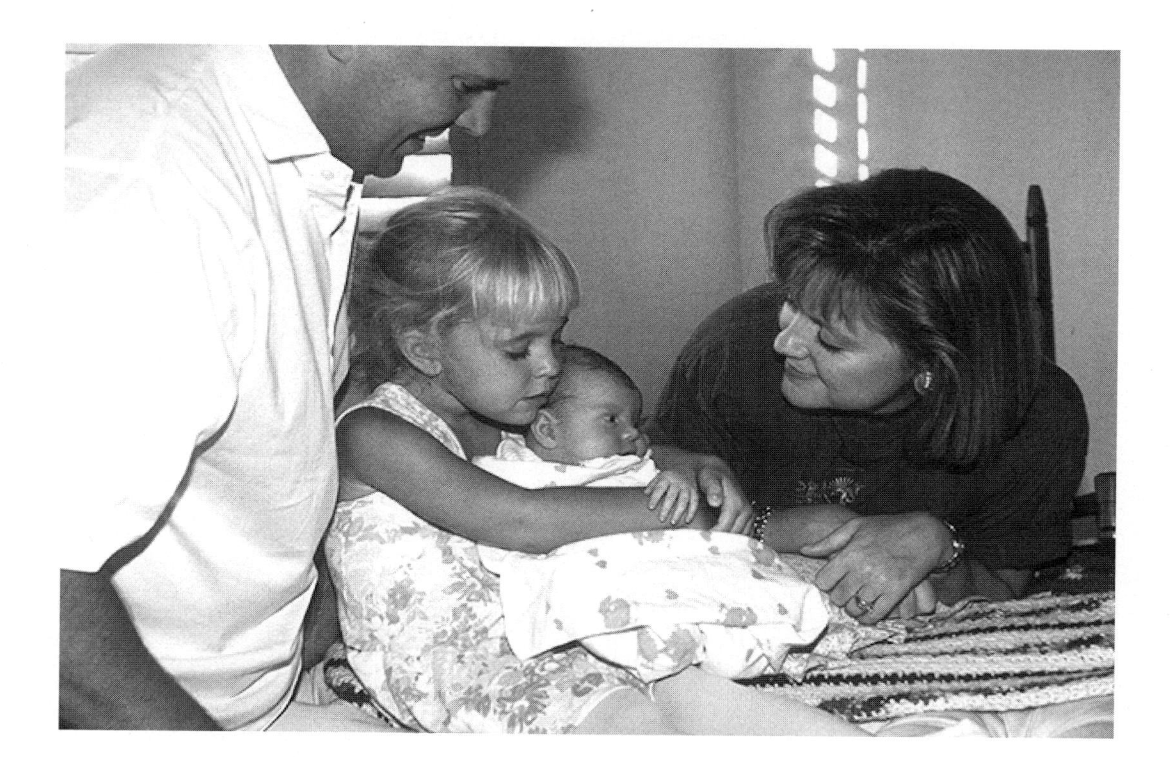

Touching brings happiness to our lives.

CHEVY

Just as there are rules in other areas of life, there are rules about our bodies.

One rule is that we should not talk about other people and their bodies in ways that might embarrass them. They need to feel good about themselves just as we do.

Also we don't need to get giggly and silly and embarrassed about our bodies and the things that bodies can do.

CHICA

Your body, after all, is not something you have to be embarrassed about.

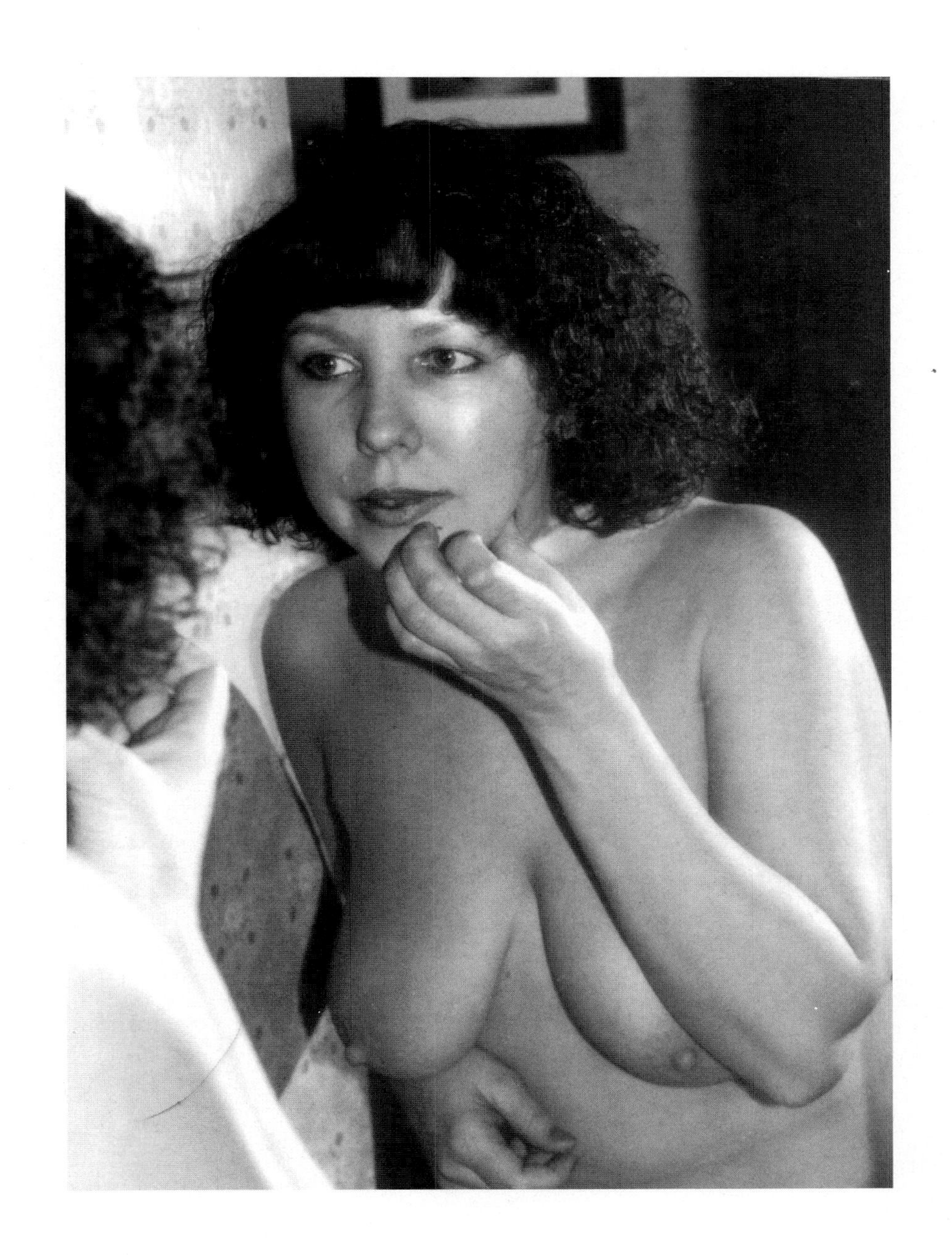

but what am I?
An infant crying in the night:
An infant crying for the light:
And with no language but a cry.

Alfred Lord Tennyson

Touching can be a problem.

Sometimes people hit each other,
or play so rough that a person gets hurt.

Also, some parts of our body are
more private than others.

An older child or grown-up may touch us
in a way that upsets us.

If any touching happens that hurts or confuses us,
we should talk about it with a grown-up we trust.

I will be the gladdest thing
Under the sun!
I will touch a hundred flowers, and not pick one.

Edna St. Vincent Milay

When everybody lives by the rules, our lives together are much happier.

One very special thing that bodies are for is having and caring for children.

Only when we are grown up and live with someone very special do we use our bodies for this.

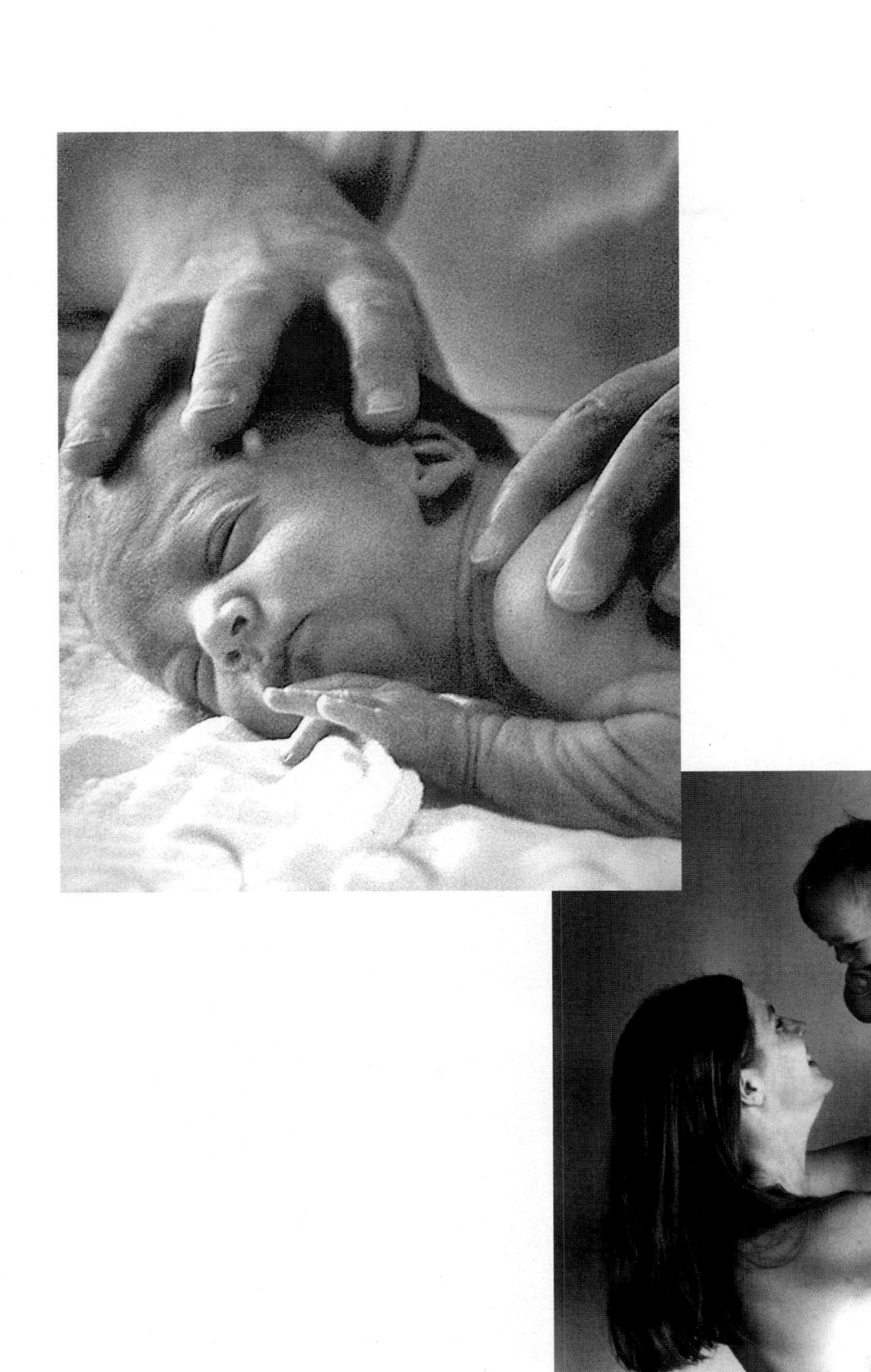

It is true?
That for me alone your love has been waiting...?

Rabindranath Tagore

There are many things you can do to be good friends with your body:

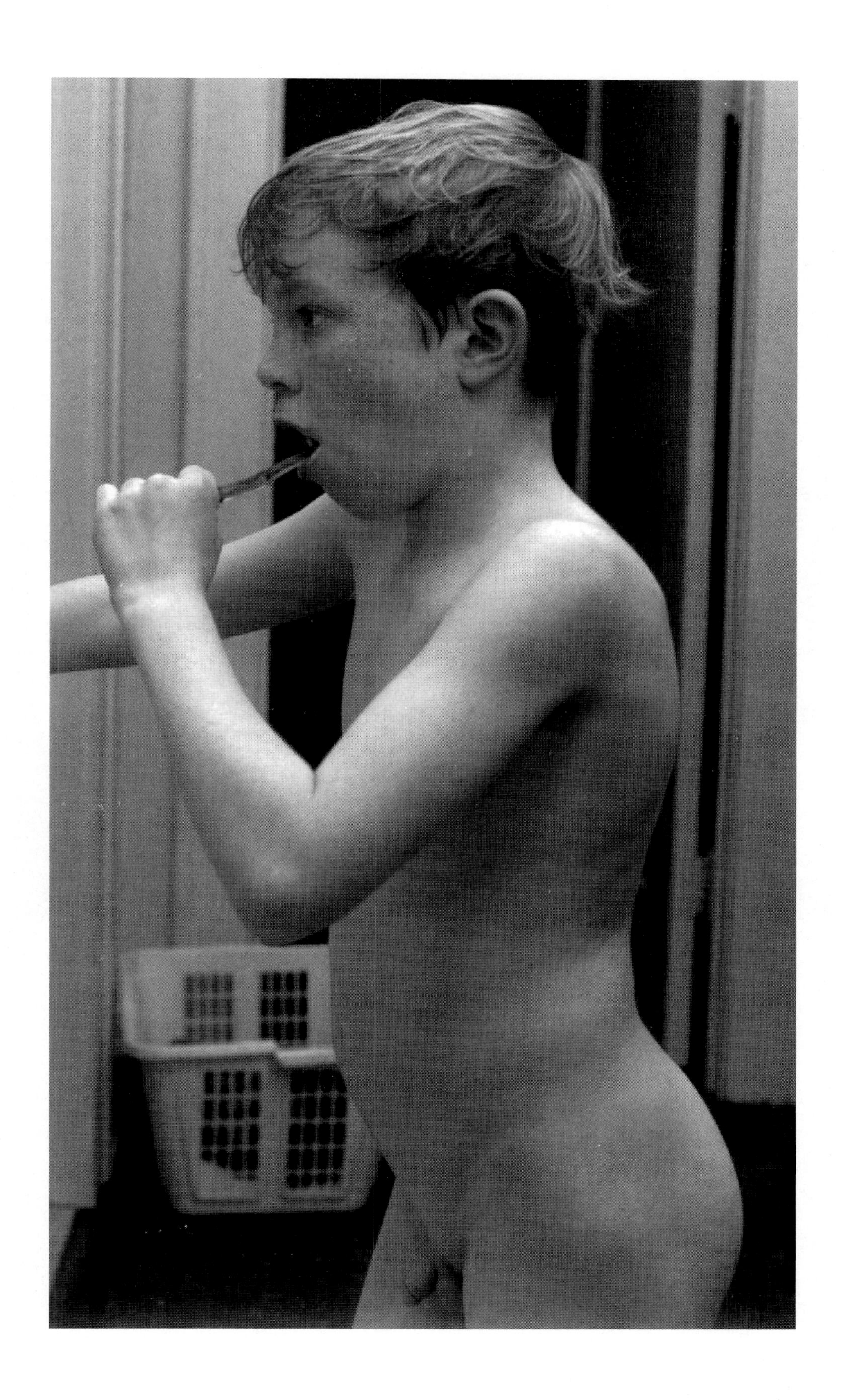

...Know that your body is *good* and beautiful. It *does* not have to be just like anybody *else's.*

...Know the rules about how others should treat our bodies, and how we should treat others.

BUGLE
BOY

...Try to follow the rules.

...Ask when you are curious about anything.

The end

Credits

Page	*Photographer*
Front Cover, 1	Jim Harrison
i, 22, 23, 34, 35, 37R, 37B, 39T, 39L, 51, 59, 71, 75	Harry Cutting
iv, 76, 77	Jim Hunter
v, 65	Norwegian Tourist Board
vi	Jean-Baptiste, *Girl with a Shell*, Samuel H. Kress Collection, ©Board of Trustees, National Gallery of Art, Washington, DC
xiii	Jean-Baptiste, *Neapolitan Fisherboy*, Samuel H. Kress Collection, ©Board of Trustees, National Gallery of Art, Washington, DC
2, 9T	Harold A. Walker
3	Gordon Schalla
4, 16	Karola Bryant
5, 32, 57	Oscar C. Williams
6, 17T, 41L, 42, 43, 68	George Bryant
7, 36T, 36B, 38L, 45T	Kay Shaw
9B, 24T, 33, 40	Fran Palumbo
10, 11, 37L	Dan P. Oberly
13	Kay Hendrich
14, 17B, 61, 63T	Bob Giandomenico
15T	Tony Rinaldo
15B, 21, 39R, 41R, 45L	John Parent
19	Charlie Palek
24B, 27, 29, 31B, 69	Derek P. Blew
25, 26B, 38B	Jan Long
26T	Xinghui Guan
28, 31T	Don Chase
30, 53, 73	Winfried Scheidges
36L, 38R	Kenneth C. Poertner
36R, 54	Tasha Hunter

Credits

41T	John Varsanyi
45R	Marilyn Iannarelli
44	Rhonda Milligan
47	Jan Isachsen
49, 67	David G. Moore
62, 63B, 64	Lola J. Reid

Poetry Credit

16	Excerpt from *Phizzog* in *Good Morning, America,* ©1928 and renewed in 1956 by Carl Sanburg, reprinted by permission of Harcourt Brace & Company
37	Excerpt from *Days* from *Collected Poems* by Philip Larkin. ©1988, 1998 by Estate of Philp Larkin. Reprinted by permission of Farrar, Straus & Giroux, Inc.
40	Excerpt from *The Little Prince* by Antoine de Saint-Exupery, ©1943 &1971 by Harcourt Brace & Company, reprinted by permission of the publisher
58	Excerpt from *Afternoon on a Hill* by Edna St. Vincent Millay, from *Collected Poems,* Harper Collins. ©1917 & 1945 by Edna St. Vincent Millay
64	2 lines (p62) from *Loves Question* from *Rabindranath Tagore: Selected Poems* translated by William Radice (Penguin Books, 1985) Translation ©William Radice, 1985. Reproduced by permission of Penguin Books Ltd.

About the Author

James Hunter, *LCSW*

Mr. Hunter is a Licensed Clinical Social Worker who received his Masters of Social Work from the University of Maryland in 1972. While he has filled a wide array of social work roles, he has stayed close to direct clinical work, supplementing his own practice with teaching and consultation. He has worked extensively with foster children and their families. Two of his special interests are adventure-based therapy and writing.

Mr. Hunter's experience includes the direct supervision of a cottage of juvenile delinquents, teaching language skills to emotionally disturbed children, overseeing the clinical aspect of a program that was concerned with the de-institutionalization of developmentally delayed individuals, social case work with a variety of client populations in assorted settings, consultation, training and clinical supervision in a number of contexts, and residential treatment, both in direct care and in administration.

Mr. Hunter has organized, taught, and presented a number of workshops, courses, and seminars relating to family therapy, parenting, crisis training, and other similar topics. He has published papers and articles in *The American Journal of Psychotherapy, Journal of Religion and Health, Journal of Pastoral Care,* and *Cognitive Therapy and Research,* among others.

Mr. Hunter is currently in private practice and also provides consultation to the Institute for the Study of Children at Risk at the University of Maine.